Dreaming
of Love

Dreaming of Love

Gil Saenz

Pentland Press, Inc.
England•USA•Scotland

PUBLISHED BY PENTLAND PRESS, INC.
5122 Bur Oak Circle, Raleigh, North Carolina 27612
United States of America
919-782-0281

ISBN 1-57197-179-3
Library of Congress Catalog Card Number 99-070725

Copyright © 1999 Gil Saenz
All rights reserved, which includes the right to reproduce this book or
portions thereof in any form whatsoever except as provided by the
U.S. Copyright Law.

Printed in the United States of America

This book of poetry is dedicated to:

All my relatives, friends, and coworkers who have been such a positive source of support and encouragement.

Table of Contents

Preface

All of the poems in this collection are related to the immense theme of love in one way or another. Love is always an important and interesting subject. It never grows old or boring. Mainly this is because it cannot be separated from any other part of life. As it has been said so often in the past, "love makes the world go around." Or as someone once told me, "love is how we all got here." Love may be something both common and trivial, and it may also be something miraculous and powerful. Poetry is an appropriate way to capture and express this contrast and all the various gradations of meaning that fall in between.

Gil Saenz
December, 1998

Dreaming of Love

Dreaming of someone who was sitting
There in the opposite chair,
Someone to talk to and to share.

I was dreaming of someone to walk with,
To share the simple beauty of nature,
And the visible world.
And yet, I usually walked alone.

I had dreamed of a night in summer,
When I was standing by the river,
With her by my side.
All the city lights reflected
On the dark, mildly, wavy waters
Giving the river a fluid, shiny look.

We had known the excitement
And the joy of being together,
And of being in love.

Night Wish

Sweetness of my life,
Come to me tonight.
Help me rest my weariness,
Refresh me with your tenderness.
We'll talk, we'll laugh,
And be at ease.
We will relax together
And do what we please.
How simple it all seems,
And yet it's only in my dreams.
So, sweetness of my life,
Come to me tonight.
Let's create some
Beautiful memories together.

Mementos

Pretty flowers tumbling through the air,
She is their fragrance and their face so fair.
The music, the candle, and the wine,
She also brings all of these to mind.

It feels like such a long time ago,
That she was my girl and I was her beau.
And in my dreams she keeps returning to me,
As my lonesome heart just won't set her free.

She is sometimes in the wind that blows
No matter what the season,
Then again, she appears sometimes
In the daylight or the moonlight
For no apparent reason.

Gazing on all the many flowers tumbling down,
I wondered at how time goes by and how a heart
Can feel love that is so profound.

How Beautiful

How beautiful is love remembered,
A love that has gone so far away.
We were so young and innocent,
But our love had already gone astray.

How beautiful is love remembered,
There was always a price to pay.
Vulnerable and open, eager to please,
Our hearts we must obey.

How beautiful is love remembered,
Kindness, goodness, and tenderness
All have their day.
The romance and fantasy of love
Brought us closer and made us
Want to pray.

How beautiful is love remembered,
Resplendent images and music
Brightened our way.
Such love remembered is more
Beautiful with every passing day.

Within the Midst

Within the midst
Of all the passing years,
Of all the people and places,
Both far and near.
Of all the winters, summers,
Autumns and springs,
Of all the feelings, thoughts,
Moments, experiences, and memories
That they bring,
Their love had somehow miraculously survived.
Just by looking into each other's eyes,
They realized how it was still
Very much alive.

Where Love Is

Love is found in many places,
And is expressed in many different ways.
It is part of all the social graces,
Of the little things we do and say.

Love is in all the natural beauty
Of the good, green earth which God has made:
A sunrise, a sunset, a mountain,
A forest, a stream, or a sparkling everglade.

Love is the great motivator,
More than just an emotion, or a feeling
To convince or dissuade.
It is a great mystery in which
The positive forces always prevail.

Summer Love

Endless summer days and nights
With warm and cool currents,
Now and again softly blowing,
Drifting along like our new found love.
Rustling leaves in the tall fertile trees,
Traced our own gently flowing feelings
Which were although quiet,
Yet still intensely warm and alive,
Stirring within us and foretelling
Of a longing that was unfolding,
Blossoming, and growing steadily
In the warmth of the summer sunshine.

Best Flower

Morning glory, oh morning glory,
Fresh as the morning dew,
Her pretty smile and youthfulness
Made me feel more youthful too.

Her simple and direct manner,
So plain and yet so true,
Gave her so much more charm
Than all the other flowers
Through and through.

Morning glory, her radiant beauty
Makes the birds sing,
And makes the pigeons coo.
I wonder if we will ever find
That special love which we
Have been seeking too.

When Love Comes Your Way

When the magic of love's golden moments
Comes into your life,
Cherish the gift and treasured times
Of that unique happiness.
Hold your lover's hand.
Embrace, kiss and be glad
That love has come your way.

Moonlight Spell

The solid white globe
That lit up the night sky
Had a magic effect.
Our imagination conjured up
A passion remembered
And places that we had been.
A full moon and her nearness,
Made me feel I had reached
The seventh heaven high.
From our evening walk
Came the song of love and romance
Under the large ivory moon
Which had cast a spell upon us.

Many Dreams, Many Loves

As sure as the seasons go by,
One after another, winter, spring,
Summer, and fall,
Our many dreams, and our many loves
Are played out on the stage of life.
Laughter, tears, pleasures, fears,
All have their part in the passion.
Just like in the movies are those times
When our dreams become a reality,
Or sometimes tragically sad and lost,
When our dreams are shattered
And unfulfilled.

Colors of Love

Love is many colors at different times.
Sometimes, love is blue from the sadness.
Then, other times, love is red
From feelings of passion and warmth.
When love is yellow, love is a lot
Of good feelings and cheerfulness.
Orange is another color of bright feelings.
When love is green, it is identified
With nature and the outdoors.
When love is purple, it is a royal feeling
For kings and queens.
The colors of the rainbow blending
Together show the happiness
And the great miracle of love.

Romantic Nights

The scent of fresh green grass
And surrounding shrubbery,
Filled the air with a pleasant aroma.

The park lights lit our path,
And made the grass an even deeper
Color of green.

For both of us as we walked along
Holding hands,
Enjoying the passing moments,
This was a special night.

We had vowed our love
To each other,
And now all we could feel
Was happiness and excitement
For the future.

Blue Melody

Searching back in my faded past
Her memory still seems to last.

I'd like to go back
And do things differently,
To have her in my life again,
For her to be a part of me.

When we were together,
We shared many simple pleasures
We had joy and happiness,
That was without measure.

Now that we've been apart so long,
The best I can do is recall it all
With a blue melody and a song.

Two Hearts

When two hearts met,
They fell in love.
They had no regret.

Their two hearts sang,
And danced, and laughed,
And soon, wedding bells rang.

Their two hearts beat
Together as one.
And, then, a third heart
Was born, and a life begun.

The miracle of two hearts
In love is full of wonder.
It is a lesson for us all
To remember and to ponder.

Friendships

One by one, slowly, carefully,
Tentative steps are taken.
Defenses begin to come down
With each new gesture,
Each new greeting,
Each new meeting,
Each new conversation.
The two move closer.
Comfortable rapport is begun.
Both persons strive to stave off
That old familiar feeling
Which we all carry around
With us now and then
Known as loneliness.

Valentine's Hope

Wishing,
Hoping and praying
For her,
And for the love
That we
Had never known.
She was
So tender
And full
Of goodness,
We deserved
Some happiness
And good things
Together.

A Beautiful Dream

Last night I dreamt we met.
We talked, we laughed and we cried.
We played and just enjoyed being together.
Nothing could and nothing would
Disturb our happiness.
The music played for us, and us alone.
It was as if we were in the Garden of Eden
And it would never come to an end.

Love Opens Every Door

There is a positive goodness that we can rarely ignore,
It is the positive power of love that opens every door.

Man's humanity to man is the ideal of evermore,
Instead God's peace and justice is what we each day
    must finally implore.

In the beauty of springtime all hearts turn to love
    which sometimes may be in store,
As love's fascination draws us all to its romantic reservoir.

Life requires struggle with opposition and a knowing
    of the score,
A striving for a balance and a moderation, and a
    harmony of once more.

Love conquers all, so it is frequently said in many books
    of yore,
It is another reminder that the positive force of love
    really does open every door.

Never Known

Kisses never known,
Embraces never shared,
Conversations never spoken,
Roses never given in love;
These are some of the saddest things,
A person unlucky in love can recall.

One heart reaching out to another,
A misunderstanding, and no love in return.
Two souls attempting to meet in the large
Universe, both on their separate sojourns.

Goodness, truth and beauty really do live,
Whether or not we personally realize them,
There is an intuition that lets us know.
It displays before us all the reality
Of the activity and aspirations of the soul
Which we sometimes forget we possess.

Flower of New Love

Her smile was like a flower in bloom,
The fragrance of our new found love
Subtly flowed forth as sweet perfume.

Rose petals freshly fell one by one.
And a tulip bud began to slowly open
As in spring is done.

The beauty of her fair and comely face
Has left a flower-like impression
On my heart
That time will not erase.

Dream Come True

Soul reaching out to another kindred soul,
Each existing in the physical world,
They were carefully observing how
Their mutual desire would finally grow.

Their prayers and thought images
Had often expressed themselves the same way.
It was a powerful feeling of drawing closer
And uniting themselves day by day.

Flowers, fragrances, sights and sounds,
Were somehow all exciting and brand new,
And their warm closeness and love
Had made their dream come true.

Maria and the Moon

It was warm that evening, and not quite June,
When Maria and I drove down by the river
To see the big, yellow, full moon.
She was talking and laughing,
Apparently in a good mood.
So too, the big, yellow moon likewise
Seemed happy and cheerful too.
The big, yellow, pale moon just suspended
In the dark nighttime sky,
Made me imagine many different,
Faraway places, times and lives.
How did this moon look over Vienna,
Athens or Rome?
Somehow it must be a little different
Than the one Maria and I
Were seeing here at home.

Summer Memento

I missed her on the first day of summer,
I was afraid I might not see her again.
It would be a long hot season without her,
How I wished we could be friends.
I missed her on the first day of summer,
I longed for what she had represented,
I longed for a love and a friend.
Warm summer days and fair skies,
Had made me stop and realize,
That the first day of summer without her,
Was not as happy as it might have been.

Love's Serenade

In love I see the sunshine bright.
In love I look forward to the night.
In love every little thing always seems right.

In love we are at the rainbow's end.
In love there is fulfillment with a friend.
In love there is always time to make amend.

In love great creations are sometimes made.
In love all music is especially played.
In love the good things rarely ever fade.

In love your smallest word or deed means so much.
In love there is a thrill in your every touch.

In love a positive inner glow pervades,
And the charm of life becomes a beautiful serenade.

Sweet Woman

Oh sweet woman how I want you so.
Oh sweet woman you don't even know.
When I see you every now and then,
I imagine your sweetness again and again.
If only somehow we could make it come true,
Friendship to love and to sweetness too.
We would bring all the barriers down,
Then we would feel our physical closeness
All around.
Sweet woman, please tell me what
I should know,
That would let me enjoy
All the sweet love that you might bestow.

Reverie

Will our paths ever cross again?
If so, I wonder when?
What does destiny hold in store,
If we should ever see each other once more?
Many years have already passed
Since the days of our youthful love
That we thought would always last.
Hoping against hope and dreaming
The impossible dream.
Trying to imagine what it would be like;
That first uncertain scene.
Winter, fall, summer and spring,
The seasons slowly pass away,
As I continue wondering
If we'll ever have our day.

The Haunted Bachelor

His nights were filled with voices,
Voices of pretty ladies
Standing outside his door.
"Am I good enough?" they would ask,
"Or how about me?" another would say.
It made him wonder, if he opened the door,
Would they really be there?
His imagination gave them an alluring
And seductive quality. Roses, perfume,
Tenderness, warmth and caring; all the good
Sides of love and romance came to his mind.
He continued to wonder.

Love is Never a Cliché

Although the subject of love
Is in all music we hear today,
It doesn't necessarily mean
That love is just a cliché.

And even if "love" is on the TV
And soap operas each day,
The freshness and beauty of love
Never becomes a mere cliché.

Either love or experience
The vacuum of negative decay.
Love is nature's way,
Of telling us how to live
With health and happiness always.

Like the air we breathe,
And the food we eat,
Love is vital and basic.
It is never simply a cliché.

Wondering

In the night air
Of the warm spring
My imagination
Keeps on wondering.
Will I find
The right love for me
This year,
Or will she be
Just another wrong choice
And insincere?
I just can't quit the notion
That there is a certain
Someone who is right for me—
Somewhere in the vast
Earthly ocean of humanity.

Forever Love

As I walked along under the weeping willow tree,
In my contemplation many memories came back to me.
A blue fantasy, some midnight rhapsodies, and
A flower of new love all made up my reverie.
Our youthful journeys had become enchanted yesterdays
Recalled with rainbow colors of love.
We had been to the paradise garden of time and forever
And witnessed the summer moon on romantic nights.
To have our dream fulfilled was our true destiny.
The words of love that we exchanged
Would follow us along on our colorful impressions.
We had lived through an incredible odyssey.

Follow Your Bliss

As we travel along on our own journeys,
Each with our own unique experiences
Going our separate distinct ways,
We must stop sometimes
To count our many blessings.
Our Heavenly Father mysteriously
Instills within us a special longing
That is with us all our days.
We long for a peace, joy and fulfillment
That is only partially attained by most.
One of our greatest gifts is our capacity
To love and to share ourselves
And our lives with others.

Emerald Eyes

Her glance had met mine,
And I had known from that time.
She was the very one,
She was the sum total
Of all my past dreams.
We had been on the grassy bank
Of the lake sitting down.
We had had long conversations
About small things.
Fully happy yet interesting,
The magic two lovers know
Had been ours for a short time.

Powder Blue

Lately my nights are very blue.
Now that I know there is someone who,
Was my sweetheart from the distant past,
And whose childish love I had held fast.

When the stars come out I look around
Hoping to share with her this blue profound.
Instead I spend my nights the usual way,
Lying quietly waiting for the new day.

Lily white flower of our childish past,
Make the nighttime colors always last.
Blend in your fair color with my blue night,
And create for us the powder blue,
Of love's happiness and love's delight.

Rose Memory

When warm breezes blow,
And summer blue skies
Hold puffy white clouds
That slowly float by,
The roses glow a rich dark red,
The color of burgundy wine,
Hanging on their green vines.

The notion of her smile
Was like one of those roses.
Many years had passed
Since they had said good-bye.
Now her rose memory always returned
Whenever he saw the roses
Hanging on their green vines.

Dreams of Tomorrow

Even when you're gone,
The eyes of the morrow,
Along that imaginary road
Keep you always on my mind.
Life is a labyrinth,
But I know that for us,
Our song of love
Will be fulfilled
With time and forever.
You are my everything.
The love rhymes,
And idyllic memories,
Were a weaving of the path
To our true destiny.

Stay With Me Always

Starlight of my every evening,
Sunshine of my every day,
You have made me very happy,
Stay with me always, stay.

Like the flowers in the garden
Blooming in the first days of May,
You came into my quiet life,
Stay with me always, stay.

You make me feel more fulfilled
In each and every little way,
So it's natural that I'm asking,
Stay with me always, stay.

If we always remain together,
And this is what I earnestly pray,
Every tomorrow will be brighter,
Stay with me always, stay.

Love's Destiny

Two separate lives,
Two separate souls,
Two separate worlds,
Two separate ships sailing along
In the sea of life,
Both wanting to be reunited,
To be together again was their prayer.
That someone, somehow could help them
And in some way,
Would transform their night into day.
Make it for real.
Their two hearts would be so happy
That their joy
They could not conceal.

Moonlight Visions

The flower, the moon, and a dream;
Driving along, I swore I saw her.
She was driving along by my side,
Or so it really seemed.
The vision, the dream, had returned
Once again, always reminding me
Of an old and special friend.
With this whole, big world
And all its teeming millions,
My heart could not forget her.
The pale yellow large moon
Was her flower,
And she was my dream.

Love Portrait

She is the magic.
She is the music, the words,
And the symphony.
She is everything to me.

Once a voice told me,
"If you really love her,
Then let her be free.
If she really loves you,
She will return, since
She will always wish
Your company."

She is my whole world.
She is all my poetry.
She is in my every fantasy.

When I recall her sweet smile,
Everything feels worthwhile.

Coquette

Sometimes it seems that she wants to play,
Then she retreats and quietly goes away.

Her apparent object is to be loved,
But that is not in reality
What she is thinking of.

How she plays the game is more important
Than what the final outcome will be.
That's why I always tend to doubt her
Sincerity.

Her appearances and deceits are so
Polished and refined,
That only an expert would be able
To detect all her hidden designs.

A Personal Treasure

Where have you gone now?
I wish I could be there.
The tender, warm embraces
That we shared
Are a lasting inspiration
To what a full relationship
Might be.
A togetherness,
A unity,
A joy,
A simple pleasure,
Sweetness and warmth,
All are a part
Of this personal treasure
That I recall.

Beautiful Flower

A rose, red and fresh
On one green stem,
And freshly cut,
Is a symbol of love,
And all other signs
Of friendship
Which are shared.

Its singular beauty
Is used to communicate
Many things
Which are not always
Best expressed
With words.

Suddenly

Suddenly before the clock
Would strike the next hour,
Before the petals softly fell from
The rose flower;
Suddenly they met, and fell in love.

This special predestined moment
Was the beginning of their dream.
Rare days and nights
Of rainbows and candlelight,
Gave their young hearts
Joy and unspeakable delight.
Now everything was theirs.

Suddenly love had come
Into their quiet lives.
She loved him. He loved her.
This they could not deny.
Love would only grow and grow
As the years would inevitably go by.

Moments In Time

The many good things we remember,
Many brief and fleeting hours,
Special times in all our lives,
As bright as the spring flowers.

Charming periods that we cherish,
Making us who and what we are,
Filled with excitement or calm,
All grown rosy and better from afar.

They are parts of our personal being,
From childhood to adult years,
Leaving on us an indelible mark
Even as their memory begins to disappear.

Summer, fall, winter, and spring,
The four seasons have their own
Rhythm and rhyme,
And always remind us of all those
Particular moments in time.

Flight of Fancy

Out of the shadows and into the dream,
My nocturnal stroll had taken me
All the way back to the reverie.
The faint faraway music
From the East had beckoned
And as the world fell away,
I had sought after that lonely woman
Who still lived in the mist of my yesterdays.
After some time I heard the nightingale,
Singing softly, as I felt myself returning
From my blissful flight of fancy.

Contact

The day our eyes met for a moment.
The day your smile touched mine.
There in the quiet gray light
Of the winter afternoon,
I felt that our souls
Had come just
A little
Closer.

She's The One

No other like her,
No one else to love,
Writing poems about her,
She's the one I was dreaming of.
Thinking about all
The many good times
We might yet have,
Living and sharing together.
No other like her,
No one else to love,
Remembering over past years
Inspirations from above.
Getting to know each other,
Appreciating ourselves in a new way,
Falling in love all over again,
Magical moments of night and day.

Autumn

The music of the wind
Brushing the leaves of the trees,
Made it all begin again.
All the memories came rushing back,
And started to unfold.

This particular season,
the wind,
and the familiar bouquet
Of the flowers,
Together recalled the story
Of all that once was ours.

Lost Intervals

Searching and looking,
Looking and searching,
Always trying to find
The part of yourself
That's been missing for a while.
It's the part of your heart,
The part of your soul,
The part of your mind
That you have somehow left behind.

She knew what you were searching for.
She knew she was a part of it all.
Searching and looking,
Looking and searching,
Trying very much to put it
All back together again.
The insight had been learned.
It didn't have to be such a struggle
After all.

Paradise Fantasy

I will wait for her
At the gates of paradise,
Where lovers may meet,
Become acquainted
And not have to apologize.

We will sit quietly
On the hilltop side by side,
While we watch the sunrise before us
And the new horizon opening wide.

Later we might pass the day
Lingering in the meadows
Savoring this brand new way.

What we couldn't do
during our earthly lives,
That is, simply be friends and lovers,
Could now come true in paradise.

The Wonder of Love

Love is music, singing, and dancing,
Laughter, joy and romancing.
Love is sharing, caring, and tender,
Patient, long-suffering, and surrender.
Love is idealistic, truthful, and beautiful,
Hardworking, diligent, and dutiful.
Love is gratitude, giving, and receiving,
Wishing, hoping, and believing.
Love is ecstasy, sadness, and pain,
Cloudy, sunshine, and rain.
Love is wonder, awe, and inspiring,
Knowing, wanting, and desiring.
Love is a great phenomenon to praise,
As it is an essential part of all our days.

Familiar Dream

Everywhere I go, everywhere I turn,
Her bittersweet memory slowly returns.
Sharing our lives, and sharing our hearts,
We walked hand in hand by the lakeside,
We were always together rather than apart.
The old familiar places,
And the old familiar faces;
How different it all seems.
All that once was our happiness
Has now become the old familiar dream.

Soaring Spirits

Piano and violin
Together blend
And fill our hearts
With pleasant joy,
While above us
In the velvet
Blue starry sky
Our spirits
Have gone to fly.

Words of Love

Words of love,
Travel through the years,
Echoing the laughter,
Echoing the tears.

Words of love,
Counting the many measures,
Reflecting the simple joys,
Reflecting the routine pleasures.

Words of love,
Recall the many enchanted hours,
Walking in the summer sunshine,
Walking in the fragrance of fresh flowers.

Words of love,
Sometimes resemble a dream,
Capturing days of rare beauty,
Capturing summer nights serene.

Words of love,
Describe two souls in love sincere,
Echoing their laughter,
Echoing their tears.

When Paths Cross

Our eye contact reminds us
Of the secret struggles
We experience
Within our souls.

Serious thoughts reflected
Upon our faces demonstrate
The unspoken conflicts
That we are living.

Morning, noon, and nighttime,
We go through an ordinary day,
We meet our fellow travelers
Who are also attempting
The pursuit of their
Own unique way.

A casual word, a glance,
Or even a smile,
Manifest the hidden, underlying
Personal drama unfolding;
All the yearning and striving,
Achieving our uncertain destinies.

Rainbow Dreams

We had gone for another walk together.
It had been one more peak moment
As we walked along in the park
Enjoying our paradise fantasy.
The beautiful flowers along our path
As well as the serenade for guitar,
Which we had overheard gave us
That just right sunset mood.
The blue mist of the early evening
Filled us with love's images,
But best of all inspired us
With those rainbow dreams.

Love's Images

Hand holding hand,
Two lovers walking in the park,
Or at the beach along the sand.
Beautiful, glowing, orange sunsets,
Sparkling vistas of exotic
Landscapes and places,
Music that somehow sounds improved,
Crowds of happy people with smiling faces,
Wine that tastes better than ever,
Secrets shared and confidences entrusted,
Happy nights of dancing for hours together,
Sweet perfume, flowers, and candlelight,
Blue skies, sunshine or clouds above,
These are some of the many
And various, images of love.

Youthful Journeys

Two souls meeting,
Two destinies greeting,
Both traveling,
Traveling along the highway of life.
They met once when they were very young,
For a short time.
Most of their lives was still
Largely ahead of them and undefined.
The first touch,
The first contact,
The first interchange had begun.
Now, they could help each other
To attain their final ultimate future,
Traveling together two as one.

Love Fantasy

We had been building castles in the air,
Dreaming a bridge of dreams,
Where we could cross over and enjoy our journey
Of unreality and happy adventures together.
Time had stood still for us
While we lived the dreamy highlife,
Tripping the light fantastic through yesterdays,
Todays, and tomorrows as we felt the bliss
And other good feelings of our love fantasy.

Dreamland

Rare imaginings came to me
Night after night.
Enchantingly beautiful women
Filled with desire
And an eagerness to please,
Were in exotic places and scenes
With picturesque surroundings.
Bright flowers of many colors,
Palm trees, sunshine and sandy,
Rolling beaches beckoned.

When Love Blossoms

Each time they meet the subtle feeling
Grows stronger.
They want their time together always
To last longer.

The music that plays within their hearts
Cannot be heard when they are apart.

Their physical and spiritual selves
Become entwined,
And they appreciate more the clouds,
The rain and the sunshine.

They desire the good of their partner
Above all,
Sharing and caring for each other,
Wonderful for the present
As well as to recall.

Blue Mist

I dreamed of a long ago time,
When our love was new
And she was all mine.
So many yesterdays, so many
Evenings, so many hours,
Filled with enchantment,
Dreams and flowers.
A beautiful memory,
All grown rosy
With the passing years,
Filled with much happiness,
But also some tears.
I've grown to exist
With only this thin blue mist
Of a past reminder.

Charm of Love

Her presence was his delight each time.
The world looked and felt better
Because she was there, close by,
And she felt the same way.
He prayed to God for her safety
And well-being both emotionally,
Physically, and spiritually.
When someone had loved him
In the way that she had shown,
He felt honor bound to return
Her love in whatever way he could.
Her happiness was his happiness.

I Wish You Many Rainbows

May your life be filled with many rainbows,
May you always have happiness and joy,
This is the wish that I wish for everyone,
Especially I wish you the miracle of love
Which time cannot destroy.

The beauty of the colors of the rainbow,
And the future happiness they represent,
I wish you all the good things that come
From those large bending arcs,
And all the things that are heaven sent.
May your life be filled with many rainbows.

Other Poetry Books by Gil Saenz:

Where Love Is
Second printing
Minnesota Ink, Inc., 1988
St. Paul, Minnesota

Colorful Impressions
Printed by
Casa De Unidad Press, 1993
Detroit, Michigan

Moments in Time
Printed by
Bookmasters, Inc., 1995
Ashland, Ohio